THE GREAT GOOD TIME

A MEMORY

ROZ KAVENEY

TEAM
ANGE
LICA

PUBLISHED FEBRUARY 2022 BY
TEAM ANGELICA PUBLISHING
AN IMPRINT OF ANGELICA ENTERTAINMENTS LTD

TEAM ANGELICA PUBLISHING
51 CONINGHAM ROAD
LONDON W12 8BS

TEAM
ANGELICA

WWW.TEAMANGELICA.COM

A CIP CATALOGUE RECORD FOR THIS BOOK IS AVAILABLE
FROM THE BRITISH LIBRARY

ISBN 978-1-9163561-8-4

To my younger self
and all other newly transitioned vulnerable women

FOREWORD

In the autumn of 2021, well into the second year of
Covid-19 and the start of the fifth year of the War On
Trans, I noticed a lot of bleakness creeping into trans
social media and thought it my job as a community elder
to remind young people that things have been, if not
worse, at least as bad in different ways.

Back in the late '70s, when I transitioned, I acquired as
my peer group a bunch of slightly younger trans women
who I met around Soho, and for a short while became
their landlady, bail person and wailing wall. I had middle
class and educational privilege they didn't – I hope I used
it for the greater good. It was – as much as my time in
Chicago – the making of me.

It taught me a lot about solidarity.

And then we all moved on. Some of them died: some of
them are still alive.

The important thing about life in an embattled communi-
ty is to have each other's backs.

The Great Good Time includes a few older poems about
that period. I've also added a selection of the work I
wrote and read for Trans Day of Remembrance and a
couple of uncollected poems from the time before I
wrote formal verse.

R.K.

CONTENTS

Memories are fabulations. Stories shift
Each time we tell them, less fact and more art
Ice splinter Clio lodges in our heart.
I thought I went there first time in a lift
That creaked a bit. Remember chandeliers
Speckled with cobweb. Not like that at all
Basement no lift but stairs no mirror ball
Floors sticky underfoot. And yet for years
I thought it otherwise but Googled it
To write these poems. What else is untrue?
I never want to find I lied to you
About these friends that time. But that's just it:
I have important things I want to say
And facts and friendship might get in the way.
We will survive their lies their hate their law
Whatever misplaced ingenuities
They will invent in an attempt to please
Their donors. We've survived all this before
Not all of us enough to tell the tale
Pass it along embellish glamourise
This is our truth although they call it lies
We call it myth or legend. Never fail
To edit decorate add artifice
It's who we are, authentic. Sequins paint
Our sparkle life. Each femme each masc a saint.
Egg cracked tale told our metamorphosis.

VIVIENNE

A broken dancer, mane of wine red hair
cell pacing pale. From time to time she'd start
to step a form from bed to wall. Her heart
brother had torn from. Should not have been there.
Did nothing. As it happens. If she had
should not. Her flutter wounded pride; her face
lost his. His blue friends threw her to this place.
Wanted to smash her. In the end they had.
Six months alone no hope. Shattered once free
white Dresden fragile. Never could quite mend
Stiff as the damaged arm she could not bend
loose in her art. And it could have been me.
Talked us free once then left. Accept the blame
that burned my cheek. Guilt sorrow naked flame

VIVIENNE 2

Knew better than to run. One more arrest.
Not a big thing. Once policemen had seemed old
Like older brother who had hurt her. Cold
the night, cell would be warm. Cough in her chest
they'd pour hot tea. They cuffed her. Cuffs were
          tight.
They stood close. Breath hot. Took her to a cell
One stroked red hair. Touched breast. She felt him
          swell
against her leg. They did not take all night.
Outside a Judas laugh told them her past.
Hair pulled. Breast punched. A fist against her jaw.
Held not in lust. For several hours more
kicked her and cursed her. Pissed on her at last.
So never trust those fine young men in blue:
They did to her. Might do the same to you.

Linda 1

The all night cinema that showed cartoons
Was where the homeless alcoholics slept
And up and down the aisles beige raincoats crept
Looking for blowjobs. Rainy afternoons
Linda would hide there. Del was on the prowl.
The tramps disliked her. Once she spilled hot tea
On an old woman accidentally
Who shouted, 'You're a man.' Her friends took up the howl
Insulted Linda left. Then she returned at night
Brought brushes bleach and dye. Quietly moved
From row to sleeping row. With care removed
Scarves bobble hats. When they put on the light
Squawking and bleary eyed in morning streets
Old men, hair pink blue gold like parakeets

Linda 2

Linda was always looking for a score.
A window vent was open. Furs inside.
Coat hangers in a waste bin so she tried
To hook a coat. And got one. Then two more.
Alarm went off. Blonde girl on roller skates
In scarlet hot pants three mink coats attracts
Attention. Cops almost had heart attacks
They laughed so hard. The court set trial dates
Weeks off. She sat there crying in a cell.
The prison doctor stopped her oestrogen.
Upset she might look like a boy again.
I took her case to the NCCL
The Guardian ran it. I will not forget
The bliss of putting that bitch in my debt.

Linda 3

Someone smashed Big Pearl's head in with a brick
somewhere on Streatham Hill. She didn't die
for several months. One open twitching eye
and halting words, and sometimes she'd be sick
trying to speak. If Linda came with flowers
Pearl would just freeze. Linda would chat away
as if there were no problem, and would say
they'll catch the bastard. Pearl would sob for hours
After she left, and never tell us why.
They both turned tricks, they both used drugs a lot.
Pearl couldn't walk, or eat, and then she got
some bug or other and we knew she'd die
and never say who'd done it. As her friend
Linda was there beside her to the end.

Linda 4

In due course Linda died. The overdose
Was probably an accident. Of course
A sentimentalist might think remorse
But I doubt that. Like most of us she chose
Living her life on her own terms. It's sad
She'd not much room for empathy. A game
She played against the world. The cards that came
To hand middling at best. One day were bad.
Friends cried. An open coffin. Stacey threw
A borrowed pen. Asked why, she said 'In Hell
She'll need to forge prescriptions.' Tale I tell
Because it has a punchline. Stacey too
OD'd. Viv smiled. A smile that showed sharp
  teeth.
'I told that girl not to catch Linda's wreath.'

Del took it personally. His small patch
Was those eight streets. He walked them every night
His sergeant said that 'though you've got a right
To chase those kids down every time you catch
Them clipping punters, there are other crimes.
It's not just them. I'd like you to arrest
The three card trick guy.' Lonely and obsessed
Del chased my friends round Soho. Several times
They hid in skips, up fire escapes. My mate
Glo up in court for clipping got the last laugh
Proved he had lied on oath. Her photograph
Of lines of sight convinced the magistrate
Who said his perjury blackened the name
Of West End Vice. He was transferred in shame

Colveston 1

The quiet intimacy of those days
Lounged on two sofas. Someone makes some tea
Someone is pulling wax off painfully
To get a stubborn hair. Some music plays
In memory it's Walking on the Moon
The soundtrack of these months because our
      friends
Hadn't yet made their albums. Music ends
And no one changes it. It's afternoon.
I try to work but don't go to my room
Roxy's complaining. Vivvy rolls a spliff
They're not quite speaking over some small tiff
About a punter. Soon they start to groom
For work. Do lips and eyes. And then they phone
A taxi. I spend my evenings quite alone

CYCLE OF VIOLENCE

Kid snatched my bag. I chased him in the rain.
Hooked him with my umbrella round the knee
Took bag back. Left him crying. Home. Made tea.
Hoped that was that. But things come round again
Inevitable. Caught me on the stairs
Three of his brothers. One a flying kick
Caught grabbed his foot. From Dad I knew the trick
Twist and he's down. Only a mad girl dares
Do that when there are three, one with a blade
Pushed kick to thigh I'm bruised. I take some blows
Dodge. They get bored and leave. Ex housemate knows.
Phone rings. Glo's voice. Offers a gun. Say I'm afraid
I won't be needing it. And pack then leave.
Fate spins the thread. We choose what life we weave.

Cadence

Walk down the street in heels. You kick them off
To run barefoot if needed. They're not cheap?
Steal the next pair. Have somewhere safe to sleep
Not your main place. And if you get a cough
Rest your hoarse voice. It might give you away.
Know every alley's exit. Cul de sac.
And trust that sense of eyes behind your back
Threaten your neck. And every single day
Sing something badly dance on blistered feet
Flirt with a squirrel. Always do your face
Even in broken mirrors. It's our place
Live full try to make every moment sweet
Drain last drops breathe deep even as the rope
Pulls. Last thing in the box is always hope.

Meard Street 1

Pam said I couldn't work there. Could not say
How much I did not want to. I'm polite.
She was apologizing. Said she might
Talk Linda and Belinda round one day.
They were the problem. Said I didn't pass
Although I had nice boobs I was too tall
Especially in heels. As I recall
Linda complained that I had a fat arse.
Belinda hated how I did my eyes
Too smudgy and my lashes weren't on straight.
Said punters wouldn't want me as a date.
It stung a little. People I despise
Whose low opinion should not weigh at all.
Mutual contempt makes everybody small.

PAM

She ran the club. Was strict. Seemed in control.
And managed this by being slightly stoned
It wasn't clear whether or not she owned
The place. If not, precisely what her role
Was money wise. I think she had a boss.
Who kept the police away, bought bad champagne.
The upstairs ceiling leaked and let the rain
Come through. I think they ran it at a loss
To launder money. Still it meant my friends
Had somewhere safe to work. Pam helped them
      save
Their pay. A sort of pimp. She gave
A fuck. Such places always have their ends.
One day the Golden Girl was locked and done.
I hope Pam grew old somewhere in the sun.

The Golden Girl Meard St W1 1982

I stare at Linda. She stares back. Such hate
As only comes with sisters. In a bar
Watered champagne the sort of men who are
Paying for your attention. It was late.
I didn't even work there. Roxy Viv
And Glo had asked me to drop round at ten.
All three had lost the front door keys again
And I was at a movie. Linda's shiv
Is in her stocking top. I have a cane
Mostly for my bad ankle. Let them go.
These little quarrels. Didn't even know.
Some snub or other. Mutual threat of pain.
Then she came back for pasta. Family.
Somehow I'm there for her and she for me.

for Stacey

Never my friend. We shared an overlap
of people and of bars. We sometimes talked
though neither of us ever would have walked
across a bar so we could talk some more.
She was the posh one. And there wasn't space
for two with cut-glass voices. She'd a face
all cheekbones and hauteur. And she was thin
though not as thin as later. Wore a dress
as the designer meant it, more or less.
While I had to accessorize at best
with belts and scarves – that time that Ossie Clark
asked who had made my outfit – in the dark –
when it was one of his. She had the ease
of looks and charm. The sort of arrogance
that puts the people round you in a trance
where they do what you want. She'd raise a brow
and waiters served her first. And men would queue
to talk to her, and pretty women too.
They bought her drinks, and clothes and pure
                cocaine
And sometimes she would smile and make her pick
of those she'd fuck. Our surgeon made her sick
and she had pain that wouldn't go away.
She paid for drugs by whoring, had to take
drugs to bear whoring. Witty, couldn't make
a joke that you'd remember the next day
She nearly died; black gunk came from her ears
and she was sick and spectral thin those years
that she had left. She spent those years content
with having little. She still had the charm

but tempered with humility and calm
and she was loved each day until she died.

Tragic farce killed her – tedious to run through
mistakes she made, and clerks and doctors too.
She lay for weeks somewhere just outside life.
Her friends around her, comforting her wife.
And one day stopped. She'd asked her closest friend
to make sure she was lovely at the end,
and paint her lips and lashes, fix her hair.
I couldn't help with that, but I was there
to witness. As I bear this witness now –
I cared, not as a friend. I don't know how
to say why. Save I feel that this is owed
to her, my chance companion on the road.

CLIPPING

Glo always said, 'You wait for them to glance
And then you smile but only with your lips.
Best not show any teeth. Don't move your hips.
Stand still. It's like a really complex dance.
They always have to lead. You can't afford
Anything they could use if it's a bust
And not a punter. Obviously you can't trust
The pigs. They lie. But take it very slow.
If it's a punter they anticipate
Get hot and bothered. Always make them wait.
They stammer slightly. Sweat. That's how you know
It's not a copper. There's that little sheen
Under their nose. Or sometimes it's between
Their eyebrows. Then they ask. And what they say
Needs to be quite explicit. Walk away
Unless they use the words. If there's two
You leave – they might be pigs – or one's the friend
Who might ask awkward questions at the end.
And when they ask how much, you first explain
That you need cash up front to get the key
And other things come later. Then you'll see
If he has fallen for it. It's a pain
But always ditch him if you're out of luck
And he suspects. He might get violent.
Not worth a beating just to pay the rent.
Wear flats. And get his cash. Then run like fuck.'

Colveston 2

Roland had moved out. Given me the keys.
Glo had got busted was in Pentonville.
I was alone and cold and slightly ill.
Listening to Brahms Piano rhapsodies
Appropriately autumnal. Pouring rain.
One in the morning. Doorbell rings. Outside
Roxy Viv. Plastic bags with all their clothes. They cried.
Viv said the Brahms was doing in her brain.
Wrapped them in towels. Made them cups of tea.
Belinda's boyfriend made a pass and threw
Them out when they refused. What could I do?
And this is how we made a family.
Hot baths. Lemon and honey for Viv's cough.
'And please Roz turn that fucking music off.'

Belinda

Belinda won the jackpot. Her sweet face
Improved a little when they did her nose.
Worked hard saved plenty. Had enough. She chose
Best surgeon she could find. Time to replace
Seedy old chasers with a hot young stud.
Richard was charming, handsome. Without fail
He cruised her friends that time she went to jail.
Seduced her mother just because he could
And let her flat. I let her stay with us.
Got patronised. Expected nothing less.
One day I met her wearing black. Distress
I'd not expected and was curious.
His oil rig had blown up and he'd fried.
She got no compensation. So she cried.

Colveston 3

We didn't like each other. Roxy moaned
Said I put too much garlic in the food.
Belinda bitched as often as she could
I was too tall too posh. And Vivvy owned
A better hair dryer and didn't share.
Glo lost it. Threw the black and white TV
Out of her bedroom window. Luckily
Hit no-one in the garden. Did we care?
Not much. Quarrels were storms blew up were done.
Swapped eyeshadow and coats. We moisturized
And looking back I sometimes feel surprised
Somehow poor angry we had so much fun
Urge to embrace as much as to compete
The witty brutal wisdom of the street.

UNWRAPPED 1982

The squat cost nothing. She worked every shift.
Every few days we'd cook huge pans of stew
Jacket potatoes pasta. This is what you do
Dreams hungers plans. Night bus or got a lift
Never a taxi. Sad men groped her tits
And sometimes paid. She'd flash a toothy smile
Knowing she'd only do this for a while
Save up and one day soon they'd change her bits
And life would start. And did. She was so proud
Removed her knickers showed us still quite raw
Purple blood bruised. She'd never wanted more
She'd earned it. Gloated. We smiled and allowed.
Our turn would come one year one month one day.
Our youngest sister first which was OK.

SISTERHOOD 1982

So many stolen glances. And the fear.
You need to know just how it was back then.
If you were trans you only wanted men
The doctor said. I saw him twice a year.
Needed his signature. I thought he'd know.
I never even thought of it at all.
Sometimes in dreams. You know how now I fall
In love so often, how my cheeks will glow
Flushed with new poems and embarrassment
When I look back, so much intensity
Between us all unspoken. Density
Emotion smoke in air. But what was meant
Could not be spoken. Rivals in our hearts
As well as sisters. If one of us starts
To say the things we have to leave unsaid
It's love that stops the conversation dead
Unspoken. But that time I was afraid
That cut we all desired would leave me numb
I'd watched Susanna climax and then come
Doing a threesome. But sometimes the blade
Will slip. These things are subtle delicate.
Glo said, 'A lot of it is in the mind
So Stacey says. You have to sort of find
A happy place and go there. Concentrate
Think waves lie back.' Late night we lay beside
Not even fingers touching. Hypnotise
Watching the friendship in each others' eyes
We breathed in rhythm. Then I gasped. And cried.

STORIES 1982

They all had stories. I felt vaguely bad.
Nothing too awful. Nothing to compare.
Roxy's dad whipped her naked on the stair.
Viv smashed her arm. Before that she had had
A place with Rambert. And the UDA
Told Glo to leave Belfast or else... Else what?
Knees drilled perhaps or maybe she'd be shot.
Which really left me nothing much to say.
That time in Manchester when I got raped
By that off duty cop whose warrant card
Meant that he had me. And his dick was hard
In virgin arse. But otherwise escaped.
Oxford punts champers. Glo's sardonic smile
Said I would get my story in a while.

For Transgender Day of Remembrance 2008

1.

It could have been me
I was young. I took risks.
True, I was white.
I hitched rides with guys
One at least was a killer
It could have been me

It could have been me
He came to my door
He showed me a badge
He pulled out a knife
He raped me. I felt
The hilt of the knife
I thought it the blade.
It could have been me.

It could have been me.
They beat me in the street
They pummelled my breasts
And tugged at my wig
And said they would burn me
It could have been me.

It could have been me
He drew up alongside
And asked me to ride
And knew who I was.
He followed my cab

And drove his car at me
It could have been me.

2.

They died
On the streetcorner with the streetlight that
          blinked
With the rubbish bin dented by a passing car
Among bricks and bent girders
On the waste ground behind the convenience
          store
In the car park behind the bar where the toilets
          flooded
And the johns were bad men. Or in bed
Their own bed where they thought they were
          safe.
They died where people who die by violence die
They died because
– Of course, there's no because. Just stupid
          whys
They died for smiling the wrong way
They died because god told someone gay things
          need to die
They died because they answered back
Or would not be called out of their names
Or let his hand go there between their legs
Or went on a hot date and told him and he didn't
          believe them until he did.
They died of other people's stupid violent
hating ways.

The ones who died
The ones we know about
Thirty a year – that's more than two a month.
Handsome young transmen murdered in their pride
Duanna, Angie, Roxy and the rest
Iraqis with their long hair shaved away
Our sisters and brothers
Thirty of them
Dead

3.

When people die
Their smiles are taken from us
Who might have seen them
And smiled back.
Their songs are taken from us
Who might have heard
And listened and been glad.
Their stories are remembered
By us, on this day

THE BAKER'S DAUGHTER

1.

It happens.
I know it happens.
We know it happens
We hope it doesn't.

It's the love
Families love us
so so very much
so much
they'd change us
fix us, twist us
cure us if they could
so that we'd come home
back to their little house
stride down the front path
barked at by the dog
purred at by the cat
and hugged by them in turn
and hugged by all of them
grandma as well
(though she was never told)
looking as we once looked
in photographs
up on the mantelpiece

so we'd be who we were
the one they thought we were
and not the one

we were inside in dreams
the one we are.

and we could go to church
with them, again
in suits and shirts and ties
hair parted at the side.

And talk to God
as God would have us talk
respecting how they think their God made us
And be with them
in heaven not in hell
dull heaven
everlastingly
in suits and shirts and ties
hair parted at the side.

Some think it's a sickness
a doctor could fix
drug the girl out of us
stir up our brain
with knives with cunning knives,
or with electrodes, shocking to the core,
or just by telling us
so many times
how sick we are.

And some of them still think
It's demons got inside us
made us change.
Such scary demons
demons of lipstick and hormones and dreams

false eyelash demons
sequins on their tails.
And if they paid a priest,
their priest enough,
he'd pray it out of us
so we would spew
demon and sequins, eyelashes and pills,
in one big vomit
and be who we were
be who they thought we were
eternally.

It sometimes happens
And it is not love.
'Love is not love
that alters where it alteration finds'
How much the less
the love that tries to change things back again
to change us back again.

Families say they love
but want to own us
want to own our souls.
Not all of them
but just the ones who try
to pull this shit,
to twist us from ourselves.

2.

It happens
And I did not always know
I gave her to them

Thirty years ago
I did not know
I had no other choice

I found her there
Little punk lilac Tiffany
Just lying there
At our front door.
God knows how she got in
Or why she came to us.

I thought it was the drugs
coz she took drugs. The blood
was trickling gently from her nose
And she was breathing, gentle fluty sighs.
And would not wake. I sent the john away
and went inside and dragged her to the couch
and called the paramedics. When they came,
they asked her name, and how I knew the kid.
All I could tell them:name and the hotel
where she'd been staying once, some weeks before,
when I went back there.

Asked if it was drugs – they didn't know.
Thought not, and they asked me
Had she some injury I knew about
To spine or brain.

Some coked up sisters
when a deal went wrong
they threw her out
out of the seventh floor,
she bounced off awnings onto someone's car

so she survived, but that was years before.
And they said, that would be the sort of thing.

Took her away.
And they went through her bag
which I had not
because I did not know
and they found her ID, her old ID,
the one that had the names of next of kin.

And that was it for me and all her friends
we couldn't visit, we weren't on the list.
Some nurse that people knew told us the rest
they shipped her back to Utah, washed
the lilac out of hair that they cut short
and combed with parting at the side.

I knew she had some friends out on the coast
and I told them. They'd done it all before
And maybe maybe maybe
Her friends,
who were our sisters
went for her
riding riding riding
on their hogs
huge Harley hogs.
Her Angel friends
and it worked out

But then I didn't know
and had no choice
and maybe saved her life
and did the right thing.

And I rang her friends
her Angel friends.
Oh God, I wish I knew.

3.

I hadn't thought of Tiffany in years
Until Melissa.

Oh fuck can you imagine how it feels
lying
drifting
out of death to wake
and out of life to sleep
pain so intense
you don't know who you are
and drugs so strong
to fight the pain
that you can't form a thought
except by inches, inches
oh so slow,
that you forget the inches as you go
and yet a thought
a thought of who you are
threads through the pain
threads through the blinding drugs,

And there's your name
you knew that it was there,
just out of reach
but someone you can hear
can kind of sort of hear
buzzing around

is calling to you by some other name
a voice you kind of know
a name you know
but not your name, the name that you claw back
a letter at a time, then lose again

Can you imagine
lying there awake
through pain and drugs
and maybe you can move
one finger half an inch
And it might be your brain
broken forever
it might be the drugs
that might wear off
right now you shit yourself
you piss yourself
you know coz you can smell
although you cannot speak, or see
or maybe hear, except that name
the name you know is wrong
calling you home.
It might be the restraints
they tied you to the bed
they mean so well
so you can't hurt yourself
ever again, so you can't do
a thing that they don't like
ever again.

And someone strokes your brow
or kisses it. And says they love you
calls you the wrong name

a judas kiss of love.
Imagine that,
and wake to that
each day, in so much pain
and know through pain and drugs
how many days
how many nights
you'll lie there out of name
and out of self and out of power to change
whatever they do to you for your good.

They keep your hair
cut short, and parted at the sides.
you feel your legs,
your elegant tanned legs
grow weak and thin.
Some day, some day quite soon
when you are strong enough,
they'd take you down and cut your breasts like hair

and you can't move
and you can't speak
you cannot even cry
but maybe turn your head
from life to sleep, from wake to death.

4.

When Stacey died
Beautiful languid Stacey
thin and frail but strong
so very strong the tumour in her brain
died of infection, poison she survived.

But not this time,
the borrowed time she had to pay again.

When Stacey died
She'd asked ages before
that we would paint her face and style her hair.
'I saw how Linda looked,' she used to say
'And it was not her best. But mine will be.'

When Stacey died,
I went along just to hold Maz's hand
I had no skill, could not be Stacey's friend
the way the others could. But nonetheless
I went there with the rest

When Stacey died
The undertaker tried to lock us out
The undertaker shouted at her friends
her wife, her parents, said that it was wrong.
He said it was the law,
she'd lived a woman, he would bury her
a man. He swore and said it was God's will
and said it was the law.

When Stacey died
The undertaker was a foolish man.
Her friends were Soho girls who worked the clubs
and worked the streets, and did not carry knives
coz knives get you arrested. Nail files though,
tail combs with metal handles, sharp enough
to show such men the error of their ways.
I had my phone, to ring a lawyer friend,
because the law – not always on their side.

Her father, old and noble, waved his cane
under his nose, and prodded at his gut
Her wife just cursed him, both in Portuguese
and in choice Hindi.

and so when Stacey died
she died
as she had lived
so elegant
so beautiful
a woman to her grave.

5.

We buried Stacey, as she would have wished
And maybe Angels rescued Tiffany
And Stacey, come to think of it, that time,
swept in in boy-drag, to the hospital
where Ruby's parents tried to lock her up
to fry the dykeness right out of her brain
And Stacey said, 'I am the one with rights
that woman's husband'
oh so butch that day
when Ruby needed her
to be the man that she had never been.
They got away,
and found themselves a justice of the peace
just to be sure.

It doesn't always go
As badly as it might
Melissa might
wake up one day

with brain and speech intact
and say, 'Why, thank you dears for your concern
and I'll be off now. Parents, you may get
a Christmas card in twenty-seven years
And doctors, you will hear
much sooner, from my lawyers.'
Sweep away and join her friends
and live, and one day laugh.

Or she
may sleep her life away
may dream a life
where they can't touch her
be amazingly
fabulously
the woman that she is
and lie there while they watch her sleep and smile
a smile that plays and mocks them on her lips.

And even if
they seem to win,
if she has lost those years
the years that never were
they tell her when they lie,
and even if
they get her home
in suit and shirt and tie
with short hair parted at the side
they'll never know
from day to day
the day that she'll wake up
inside the body they have forced on her
and be so angry

oh they will not like
Melissa when she's angry
or Tiffany
when she is mad

Those girls'll Samson-smash
the preacher's church
dull heaven of their gods
and hospitals
where doctors sell their skills
to twist their patients
from their proper selves,

And they will destroy
the little houses
with the dog and cat
lazing upon the porch.

Their families
whose love is selfishness
whose truth is lies
Will never know
until the day
the day when it will come
the curses she is muttering in her sleep
the curses brothers, sisters chant along.

Curses whose day, however long delayed,
will rescue her. will bring our sisters home.

FROM THE HOUSE OF THE DEAD

1.

I lay
burning
fragile.
White skin of pain
drawn
flushed
pink skin of fever.
Changing of season.
Under the skin
poison surged.
Where I am hollow
filled
yellow grey stink.

Every eight minutes
I could press
the button of relief
sleep's other sister
not death
loss of my companion
pain.
Agony's leaving
slow withdrawing tide.

Blank
sleep pain and Fetanyl
and Liszt
Hungarian Rhapsodies on repeat
round and round and thud and swell.

Possessed
sleep pain and music.
Mostly
I was somewhere else.

She hovered
the nurse
not nursing
muttering
comminations
exorcisms
prayers like scourges
curry brushes
who would have burned me if she could.
Her pastor said I was
unclean
possessed
seven demon inhabited,
swept and garnished

She was there to wash
to bathe
to drip
water from ice
Instead
Prayer and no touch
unclean possessed
danger to touch
danger to souls
a danger to her soul
her pastor said.
And I survived
my fever

and his Christian hate.
But this is how we die.

2.

We die
We shatter at a touch
Prince Rupert's drops
dark glass bead
single sweet spot
that breaks us into shards.

Fragile – everyone
is fragile
yet we break
we die
lie broken.
So many of the few of us.

They didn't test her for a second drug
they waited for the fit to go away
forgot to check the withered fragile vein
they left him in the room for hours alone
thought the small ulcer was the only one
and so we die

forgot
left
assumed
failed
waited
left
and this is how we die.

3.

But do not die alone
surround
our friends and sisters
brothers lovers
write their names
in books of hours, books of days,
books of devotion
illuminate
and decorate

hours, days, devoted by the bed

Ask, wipe the face
ice-cool fever
love and remind
and never pray
never pray as they do
just whisper
our names
and call us out of pain.
And hold our hands
hold us as we wake
and hold us if we die

fragile
not alone.
And this is how we die.

SESTINA OF MOURNING

Never forget, they kill us on the street
and most of us they kill are black and brown
It's true that if they could they'd kill us all
In this time and this place we're safe to mourn
Our sisters' deaths whose lives were never safe
Their lives our war they fought on the front line

When I was young, I walked that street, that line
My friends and teachers taught me on the street
My life when older happens to be safe
Mostly because I'm white, not black or brown
And it's my younger self I also mourn
I could have been them, so I mourn them all

Bad men may try, but cannot kill us all
We know our history, of the long line
brothers and sisters, all of those we mourn
not just the ones who fell upon the street
this year but all who white, yellow, black, brown
died in that past when none of us were safe

We have this moment here when we are safe
Which may not last. Because they hate us all
the rich white us, not just the black and brown
We stand here linking arms in a long line
with our dead sisters, live ones on the street
Never forget to honour and to mourn

It is political to stand and mourn
in silence. We can do this, we are safe

And yet they also mourn out on the street
Blow on their hands in cold, and cry. They all
know that each death is one in a long line
and most of those who die are black or brown

Never forget them. Sisters black and brown
most of the names on the long list we mourn
This day is not about some perfect line
one of us gets to write because we're safe
And some of us are rich, and it's true all
of us are here not working on the street

Black white and brown, in danger or quite safe
We have to mourn our sisters, mourn them all
In solidarity's unbroken line, rich poor, or standing proud
            out in the street

For Transgender Day of Remembrance 2014

Remember deaths. Also remember lives
of which death both is and really is not part.
Think of it long enough to break your heart.
And talk of guns and clubs and stones and knives.

Then call a halt, and sing, eat, laugh and dance,
as they would do if here. They'd see us cry.
Not knowing they are dead, would wonder why.
So celebrate for them. We have the chance

which they don't anymore. They partied hard.
Drank when they could afford it. When their luck
was good, sometimes enjoyed a cheerful fuck.
Were happy often. Sometimes found a yard

red silk, blue cotton, cut or wrapped a dress
that looked so fine, you'd see them and shout
        Yes!

Ridley Road 1981

Glo in black silk under a leather coat
Crushed hat over one eye. She's platinum
Teased with a tail comb white cloud. And we come
Vivvy the redhead, scarf around her throat
High step her fluid gestures legs and arms
Knee warmers and that single awful scar
Her elbow. Roxy's sultry smirk. We are
Buying late night kebabs. And never harms
Come near us for they wouldn't fucking dare.
Protected by the nothing left to lose
Sisters in cuts and pills and all we choose.
I'm young thin quite good looking and was there
And am in memory transformed to rhyme
This lasting fragment of the great good time

Also available from Team Angelica Publishing

Prose

'Reasons to Live' by Rikki Beadle-Blair
'What I Learned Today' by Rikki Beadle-Blair
'Faggamuffin' by John R Gordon
'Colour Scheme' by John R Gordon
'Souljah' by John R Gordon
'Drapetomania' by John R Gordon
'Hark' by John R Gordon
'Fairytales for Lost Children' by Diriye Osman
'Cuentos Para Niños Perdidos' – Spanish language edition of
        'Fairytales', trans. Héctor F. Santiago
'Black & Gay in the UK' ed. John R Gordon & Rikki Beadle-Blair
 'Sista! – an anthology' ed. Phyll Opoku-Gyimah, John R Gordon &
        Rikki Beadle-Blair
'More Than – the Person Behind the Label' ed. Gemma Van Praagh
'Tiny Pieces of Skull' by Roz Kaveney
'Fimí sílè Forever' by Nnanna Ikpo
'Lives of Great Men' by Chike Frankie Edozien
'Lord of the Senses' by Vikram Kolmannskog

Playtexts

'Slap' by Alexis Gregory
'Custody' by Tom Wainwright
'#Hashtag Lightie' by Lynette Linton
'Summer in London' by Rikki Beadle-Blair
'I AM [NOT] KANYE WEST' by Natasha Brown

Poetry

'Charred' by Andreena Leeanne
'Saturn Returns' by Sonny Nwachukwu
'Selected Poems 2009-2021' by Roz Kaveney